WILD ABOUT ANIMALS

GIANT PANDAS

By Martha London

Kaleidoscope
Minneapolis, MN

The Quest for Discovery Never Ends

This edition first published in 2020 by Kaleidoscope Publishing, Inc.

For information regarding permission, write to
Kaleidoscope Publishing, Inc.
6012 Blue Circle Drive
Minnetonka, MN 55343

Library of Congress Control Number
2019938835

ISBN
978-1-64519-003-5 (library bound)
978-1-64494-245-1 (paperback)
978-1-64519-103-2 (ebook)

Printed in the United States of America.

Bigfoot lurks within one of the images in this book. It's up to you to find him!

TABLE OF
CONTENTS

CHAPTER 1

In the wild, pandas only live in China.

Slow and Steady

Fog settles in the mountain forest. Pine trees and bamboo reach for the sun. Poking above the mist are two black ears. The panda sits among the bamboo shoots. He's an adult. The panda weighs more than 220 pounds (100 kg).

Bamboo is delicious. But it doesn't give the panda much energy. He can't **digest** most of the bamboo he eats. That means he has to eat a lot of it. Each day, the panda spends about twelve hours eating. He needs to eat 25 pounds (12 kg) of bamboo. The rest of his day is pretty lazy. He spends most of the remaining hours sleeping.

The panda wanders around his **territory**. He doesn't need a lot of space. Pandas like to live by themselves. There are other pandas nearby. He can smell where they marked the pine trees. His space overlaps with other pandas. But he doesn't see them very much. They try to stay out of each other's way.

His feet pad through the grass. Dew collects in his fur. It is cool and wet in the mountains during the spring. But there is also plenty to eat. The panda finds a good spot. He plops down in the grass. Around him is lots of bamboo. It is tender and green. It is excellent for chewing on. He crunches on the stalks. Even in the winter, the panda **forages**. He eats bamboo all year. In the spring, he eats the tender shoots and leaves. But during the winter, the bamboo stops growing. When snow blankets the ground, the panda pulls up bamboo. He chews on the roots.

FUN FACT

Pandas are good swimmers.

Pandas mostly eat bamboo. They sometimes eat birds and small rodents, too.

PANDA DIETS

Like all bears, pandas eat meat and vegetables. They eat a lot of bamboo. But bamboo does not give them a lot of energy. They cannot chase animals. More than one million years ago, pandas ate mostly meat. They still have stomachs made for meat. Scientists think pandas' main source of **prey** died out. Pandas had to find a new food source.

PARTS OF A GIANT PANDA

The panda is exhausted from eating. It is time for a nap. He stretches out on his back. The fog lifted a couple hours ago. The sun is bright in his eyes. A bird calls from a tree to his right. An animal rustles in the grass. He crosses his arms over his eyes. When he wakes up in three hours, he will be hungry. Luckily, there is a big patch of bamboo next to him.

FUN FACT

Pandas produce more than 40 pounds (18 kg) of waste per day.

Pandas sleep for most of the day.

CHAPTER 2

Why Black and White?

Snow covers the ground. A panda blends into her surroundings. She is not like most bears. Her cousins' coats are shades of brown. Hers has a pattern. She is black and white. Her legs and shoulders are black. Her face and back are white. On her face, she has two black circles around her eyes. Her ears are also black.

In the middle of winter, most bears sleep. But pandas don't. They can't eat enough bamboo to sleep through the winter. They need to keep eating.

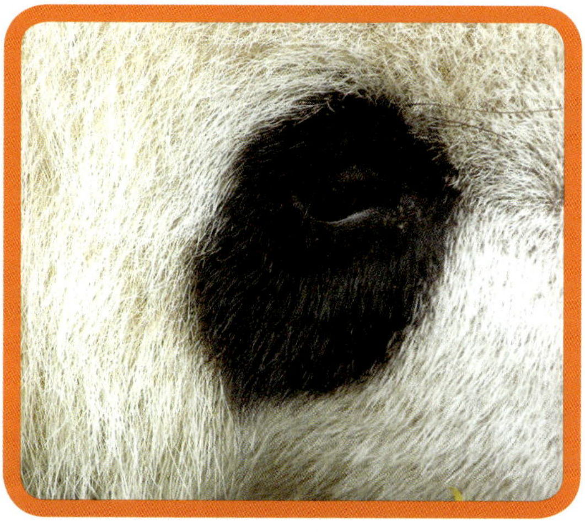

A panda's white fur blends into snow.

A panda's black fur blends in with trees and shadows.

Some animals' coats change color. They shed their summer coats for white fur in the winter. But pandas cannot do that. Pandas change climates often. Their fur cannot change fast enough. So pandas developed a different solution. Their coats keep them hidden all year long. Pandas like to stay in the shadows.

The panda takes a nap in the snow. She makes a nest and curls up. Around her, trees and dried bamboo rise up. Long lines of shadows look like the stripe on her shoulder. Her white fur blends in with the snow.

As the months pass, the snow melts. New bamboo starts to grow. Everything is green and growing. But the panda still blends in. The sun shines down through the trees. Lines of light and shadow spread through the forest. In between the light and dark, the panda is able to hide.

The panda's dark circles around her eyes are important. But they are not for hiding. Each panda has unique black circles. She recognizes different pandas that pass through the forest. Their circles are like fingerprints. Each panda is a little different.

FUN FACT

Giant pandas have the second-longest tails in the bear family.

No two pandas have the same markings on their eyes.

CHAPTER 3

At Home in the Forest

A mother panda holds her cub. The baby has thin white fur. He hasn't grown his black and white coat yet. He is two weeks old. His fur will grow when he is a month old.

The mother takes care of her baby. He cannot see. He cannot move on his own. He won't start crawling around for another two months. When he was born, the mother held him for days. She did not leave the **den**.

FUN FACT
A newborn panda is about the size of a stick of butter.

Pandas are the smallest mammals at birth in comparison to the mother's size.

A full-grown male panda can weigh up to 300 pounds (136 kg).

The cub grows. He follows his mother around. They go looking for tasty bamboo. He starts eating bamboo when he is six months old. But he still gets **nutrients** from his mother's milk. Three months later, he will stop drinking this milk completely.

HOW BIG ARE GIANT PANDAS?

Giant pandas can grow up to **6 FEET (1.8 M)** long!

Young pandas learn to climb trees from their parents.

He explores the hills. This is when he learns important skills. His mother teaches him to climb trees. He falls a lot. Sometimes he rolls down the hill. But he's okay. During the winter, he plays in the snow. The panda's thick fur protects him. His mother plays with him.

The cub stays with his mother for a long time. He lives with her for two years. Then he goes off on his own. But he is still growing. He won't be fully grown until he is six years old.

Pandas are good climbers.

CHAPTER 4

Pandas Need Help

Central China has large, towering mountains. Pandas live in high **elevations**. They spend their time 5,000 feet (1,500 m) above sea level. High in the mountains, pandas are safe. They used to live farther down the mountain. But their forests were destroyed. Farmers needed the land to plant **crops**. So pandas moved up the mountain.

Pandas face habitat loss because of humans.

Panda populations are slowly growing. But they are still **vulnerable**. People destroy their forests. They have less space. Less space means less food for pandas to eat. It is important to protect panda **habitats**. Pandas live for twenty years in the wild. But mothers raise their cubs for a long time. A mother only has five or six cubs in her lifetime.

Where Do Giant Pandas Live?

Scientists believe pandas will be okay. It helps that the people in China love pandas. They want to protect these important animals. But protecting them takes hard work.

Pandas live in a very small part of China. The government created reserves to help pandas. Reserves are spaces set aside for a specific use, such as protecting panda habitats. There are sixty-seven panda reserves in China.

FUN FACT

The World Wildlife Fund logo is a panda. It was inspired by a panda named Chi-Chi.

People all over the world love pandas.

Zoos are also helping pandas. It is hard to study pandas in the wild. But scientists learn more about pandas at zoos. This helps them understand what pandas need to survive in the wild.

Many zoos have panda breeding programs. Pandas born and raised in zoos cannot be released in the wild.

All pandas in zoos are borrowed from China.

But they still help scientists. Animal **conservationists** want to see pandas live long and healthful lives. With hard work, scientists believe pandas can thrive.

BEYOND THE BOOK

After reading the book, it's time to think about what you learned. Try the following exercises to jumpstart your ideas.

THINK

DIFFERENT SOURCES. Think about what types of sources you could find on panda habitats. What could you find in an encyclopedia? Would that be different from an interview with a zookeeper? How could each of the sources be useful in its own way?

CREATE

SHARPEN YOUR RESEARCH SKILLS. Pandas used to live at the bottom of mountains. But habitat destruction forced them to move to higher elevations. Where could you go in the library to find more information on the impact of habitat destruction on animals? Who could you talk to who might know more? Create a research plan. Write a paragraph about your next steps.

SHARE

SUM IT UP. Write one paragraph summarizing the important parts of the book. Make sure it's in your own words. Don't just copy what is in the text. Share the paragraph with a classmate. Does your classmate have any comments on the summary? Do they have additional questions about pandas?

GROW

DRAWING CONNECTIONS. Create a drawing that shows the connections between pandas and bamboo forests. How do the forests affect the way pandas eat, sleep, and live? Think about how learning about bamboo forests could help you better understand pandas.

RESEARCH NINJA

Visit www.ninjaresearcher.com/0035 to learn how to take your research skills and book report writing to the next level!

RESEARCH

DIGITAL LITERACY TOOLS

SEARCH LIKE A PRO

Learn about how to use search engines to find useful websites.

FACT OR FAKE?

Discover how you can tell a trusted website from an untrustworthy resource.

TEXT DETECTIVE

Explore how to zero in on the information you need most.

SHOW YOUR WORK

Research responsibly—learn how to cite sources.

WRITE

GET TO THE POINT

Learn how to express your main ideas.

PLAN OF ATTACK

Learn prewriting exercises and create an outline.

DOWNLOADABLE REPORT FORMS

Further Resources

BOOKS

Bell, Samantha S. *Giant Pandas Are Awesome*. 12-Story Library, 2018.

Daly, Ruth. *Bringing Back the Giant Panda*. Crabtree Publishing, 2019.

Herrington, Lisa M. *Giant Pandas*. Scholastic, 2019.

WEBSITES

FACTSURFER

Factsurfer.com gives you a safe, fun way to find more information.

1. Go to www.factsurfer.com.
2. Enter “Giant Pandas” into the search box and click .
3. Select your book cover to see a list of related websites.

Glossary

conservationists: Conservationists are people who work to protect natural resources. Conservationists work to save panda populations.

crops: Farmers plant crops to grow food. Farmers grow crops in land that pandas used to live in.

den: A den is a shelter that animals use when they give birth. A mother panda stays in the den with her cub.

digest: To digest food, the food goes through the stomach. It is very hard for a panda to digest bamboo.

elevations: Elevations describe how far above the sea a piece of land is. Pandas live in elevations higher than 5,000 feet (1,500 m).

forages: An animal forages when it looks for food. The panda forages for food and then sleeps.

habitats: Habitats are a place where animals live. Panda habitats are threatened by humans.

nutrients: Food has nutrients that give animals energy. Bamboo doesn't have a lot of nutrients for pandas.

prey: Prey is an animal that another animal eats. Scientists think pandas' prey died out, so now they eat bamboo.

territory: A territory is the area an animal lives in. A panda's territory is small.

vulnerable: An animal is vulnerable when it is in danger of being hurt. Forest destruction makes pandas vulnerable.

Index

PHOTO CREDITS

The images in this book are reproduced through the courtesy of: Anton Watman/Shutterstock Images, front cover; Eric Isselee/Shutterstock Images, pp. 3, 6, 30; Arnaud Champion/Shutterstock Images, pp. 4–5; Bryan Faust/Shutterstock Images, p. 7; irakite/Shutterstock Images, pp. 8, 25; Foreverhappy/Shutterstock Images, pp. 9, 21; Julie119/Shutterstock Images, p. 10; Gerard Lacz/Science Source, pp. 10–11; clkraus/Shutterstock Images, pp. 12–13; Wonderly Imaging/Shutterstock Images, p. 13; asharkyu/Shutterstock Images, p. 14; Niti Tangpaitoon/Shutterstock Images, pp. 14–15; plavevski/Shutterstock Images, pp. 16, 16–17; SJ Travel Photo and Video/Shutterstock Images, p. 18; Chipmunk131/Shutterstock Images, p. 19 (person); apple2499/Shutterstock Images, p. 19 (panda); Hung Chung Chih/Shutterstock Images, pp. 20, 26–27; Fernan Archilla/Shutterstock Images, pp. 22–23; Djohan Shahrin/Shutterstock Images, p. 23; Red Line Editorial, p. 24.

ABOUT THE AUTHOR

Martha London is a writer in Minnesota. She's never met a panda, but when she was four, she fed marshmallows to black bears.